"Kathryn Butler has provided the church with a treasure in *What Does Depression Mean for My Faith?* Combining her clinical training and her own lived experience of depression, she offers depressed Christians, their pastors, and fellow congregants invaluable help, steering a course through depression. This resource is indispensable for anyone navigating the theological questions that surround depression."

Karen Mason, Director of Hamilton Counseling Program, Professor of Counseling and Psychology, Gordon-Conwell Theological Seminary

"*What Does Depression Mean for My Faith?* is an incredibly helpful resource, full of clinical insight, practical wisdom, and biblical truth. Kathryn Butler writes with great tenderness and care, always with a view toward the hope we have in Christ. Her words meet us in the dark and point us to the light."

Scott James, MD, author, *The Sower; The Expected One; Where Is Wisdom?;* and *When Your Child Is Ill: Nurturing Faith in Hard Times*

"This book is compassionately tailored to those crushed by both depression and the gnawing fear that their depression excludes them from the hopes of their faith. While Dr. Butler and I come at the issue of depression from different angles, I love her practical tools for walking faithfully as a Christian in the face of severe depression. Full of scriptural perspective on weathering the storm, this book encourages hurting strugglers toward Christ!"

J. Alasdair Groves, Executive Director, Christian Counseling & Educational Foundation; coauthor, *Untangling Emotions*

T0327149

"What a beautifully balanced book about depression and faith. Kathryn Butler writes with a rare combination of biblical and medical wisdom, providing sufferers with a hope-filled and practical road map to healing."

David Murray, Pastor, First Byron Christian Reformed Church, Byron Center, Michigan; author, *Christians Get Depressed Too* and *Why Is My Teenager Feeling Like This?*; coauthor, *A Christian's Guide to Mental Illness*

What Does Depression Mean for My Faith?

TGC Hard Questions

Jared Kennedy, Series Editor

Does God Care about Gender Identity?, Samuel D. Ferguson
Is Christianity Good for the World?, Sharon James
What Does Depression Mean for My Faith?, Kathryn Butler, MD
Why Do We Feel Lonely at Church?, Jeremy Linneman

What Does Depression Mean for My Faith?

Kathryn Butler, MD

CROSSWAY®

WHEATON, ILLINOIS

What Does Depression Mean for My Faith?

© 2024 by Kathryn Butler

Published by Crossway
1300 Crescent Street
Wheaton, Illinois 60187

Published in association with the literary agency of Wolgemuth & Associates.

Cover design: Ben Stafford

Cover image: Unsplash

First printing 2024

Printed in the United States of America

Trade paperback ISBN: 978-1-4335-9345-1
ePub ISBN: 978-1-4335-9347-5
PDF ISBN: 978-1-4335-9346-8

Library of Congress Cataloging-in-Publication Data

Names: Butler, Kathryn, 1980– author.
Title: What does depression mean for my faith? / Kathryn Butler, MD.
Description: Wheaton, Illinois : Crossway, 2024. | Series: TGC hard questions | Includes
    bibliographical references and index.
Identifiers: LCCN 2023037322 (print) | LCCN 2023037323 (ebook) | ISBN
    9781433593451 (trade paperback) | ISBN 9781433593468 (pdf) | ISBN
    9781433593475 (epub)
Subjects: LCSH: Depression, Mental—Religious aspects—Christianity.
Classification: LCC BV4910.34 .B88 2024 (print) | LCC BV4910.34 (ebook) | DDC
    248.8/625—dc23/eng/20231211
LC record available at https://lccn.loc.gov/2023037322
LC ebook record available at https://lccn.loc.gov/2023037323

Crossway is a publishing ministry of Good News Publishers.

BP			33	32	31	30	29	28	27	26	25	24
15	14	13	12	11	10	9	8	7	6	5	4	3	2	1

Contents

What Does Depression Mean for My Faith? *1*

Acknowledgments *45*

Notes *47*

Recommended Resources *57*

Scripture Index *59*

SARAH, A FAITHFUL Sunday school teacher who enthralls kids with stories about God's goodness, misses several weeks of church. When friends reach out, she admits she's tired, but she offers little other explanation and excuses herself from conversations. Loved ones observe that she seems withdrawn, as if a light within her has gone out.

Then, Sarah suddenly resigns from teaching Sunday school. Though at first she's reticent to admit her struggles, she eventually confides that she's overwhelmed with despair, can't concentrate, and no longer finds joy in the things she loves. She fears that her inability to overcome her depression with prayer and Bible study disqualifies her from teaching children Scripture. "How can I teach about God's love when I can't feel it myself?" she says through tears. "I know the gospel, yet I can't pull myself out of my sadness. I'm a hypocrite." Sarah's doctor has prescribed an antidepressant, but she feels deep-seated shame that she needs medication for a spiritual matter. The longer

Sarah talks, the more her thoughts turn toward her doubts about whether God hears her prayers for relief, whether he loves her, and whether she can really be a Christian if she's wrestling through the darkness of depression.

Studies suggest that no matter where in the world we live, we'll at some point encounter people like Sarah who struggle with a debilitating, pervasive joylessness. While the dynamics at play are complicated, reflecting a tangled web of neurological, physical, social, and emotional factors, distinctly spiritual effects can arise for someone who experiences depression. What does depression mean for such a person's faith, and how can church leaders respond lovingly to those among us who face such a dark, unsettling, and sometimes baffling dilemma?

The term *depression* can generate confusion. When used too loosely, it can be associated with feelings of grief and sadness that are appropriate responses to the brokenness in our world. The Bible is replete with scenes of the aggrieved weeping and tearing their robes, lamenting over terrible loss and hardship (Job 3; Pss. 13:1–3; 22:1–2; 69:1–3). Even our Lord wept, first for the departed Lazarus (John 11:33–36), then over Jerusalem (Luke 19:41–42), and finally as the man of sorrows whom the prophets foretold

(Isa. 53:3; Matt. 26:36–46). Such examples reveal that our tears are God-given. As they dampen our faces, they provide a balm for our wounded hearts and point to our need for a Savior.

Clinical depression—also called *unipolar depression* or *major depressive disorder*—differs from this ordinary sorrow. Typical grief unfolds in stages, with healing eventually occurring over time. The same is true when we experience momentary seasons of loss or discouragement, or even trials that challenge our faith. Such circumstances may temporarily cripple us, but new growth springs from the bruised stems. The wounds heal, and the darkness does not stay.

By contrast, clinical depression (hereafter in this book called *depression*) is a pervasive disorder of mood and thought that deadens joy. Tears flow for too long, and for reasons we can't pinpoint. No matter how earnestly we strive to free ourselves from the depths, each day dawns bleaker, and the things that once inspired awe and delight lose their imprint. As pastor Todd Peperkorn describes in his raw and poignant memoir on depression:

> It is a frightful disease of the mind, turning one inward, sucking out the very marrow of a personality, until

3

there is nothing left but darkness. It is a great weight that never lets up, never releases the sufferer from its crushing power.[1]

The mechanisms behind this "great weight" are complex and heterogeneous, as we will discuss. Whatever the causative factors, the effects of depression are so disabling that questions of faith become fundamental. The brain changes that affect mood, outlook, and concentration in depression can also impair enjoyment of God's grace. As Christians, we delight in our salvation through Jesus's sacrifice, but depression swallows up our very capacity to delight. The gospel may ring familiar, but we fear that grace has withered away and God has withdrawn from our reach. We may acknowledge the truth in Christ, but as gloom hollows out our hearts, we cannot *feel* the truth. We grapple in the dark, our hearts heavy as lead, and the enemy hisses into our ears: "God doesn't love you. He's forgotten you. You're worthless. You don't matter. *Nothing matters.*"

In such bleak times, sufferers of depression need Christian love and the truth of the gospel more than ever. And in such times, pastors, elders, teachers, church leaders, and even lay members may find themselves guiding disciples through some harrowing questions:

- "I know the gospel. I should have joy in Christ. Does my depression mean I don't have enough faith?"
- "Why is God allowing me to suffer this way?"
- "I've prayed and prayed for relief from this. Why hasn't God answered?"
- "My doctor says I should go on an antidepressant, but is it right to take medication for this?"
- "The idea of dying feels easier than living right now. What hope do I have?"
- "I'm not worthy of God's love. Why should I even carry on?"

As a physician familiar with the technicalities of depression and as a sufferer intimate with its subtleties, I hope this booklet will equip church leaders to respond to such questions with wisdom, truth, and compassion. I also hope the following discussion reassures sufferers that nothing—not even the shadows of depression—can wrench them from God's love in Christ. Toward these ends, this book offers a clinical overview of depression, a biblical survey of suffering, practical guidance on how to support Christian brothers and sisters, and encouragement for those struggling in the dark. My prayer is that this book will help reaffirm Christ's love for the suffering, prepare church leaders to guide the afflicted, and help both to cleave to the life-giving hope and light of Christ's love.

More than "Feeling Down": A Clinical Overview of Depression

Like other mental illnesses, clinical depression is a hidden disability. It leeches all light from life but does so without visible scars. It skulks behind everyday routines. We go to work and pick up our kids from school but fight to breathe. We force a smile while our regard for life erodes away. As Charles Spurgeon described, "The flesh can bear only a certain number of wounds and no more, but the soul can bleed in ten thousand ways, and die over and over again each hour."[2]

In this section, we'll discuss the epidemiology, causes, clinical characteristics, and treatment of depression, to help cultivate an understanding of this disabling condition. The goal isn't to overwhelm you with medical jargon but rather to offer insight into the high prevalence of depression, its complexity, its power to disable, and effective treatments so that when faced with questions, you can respond with sympathy, confidence, and wisdom.

Epidemiology

Depression is especially common in the US, with a twelve-month prevalence of 10 percent and a lifetime prevalence of 21 percent nationwide,[3] but the condition by no means restricts itself to American shores. On the contrary, it afflicts three hundred million adults worldwide, approximately 4 percent of the global population.[4] Studies estimate a twelve-month prevalence of 5 percent[5] and a lifetime prevalence of 12 percent across continents.[6] Such statistics hint that no matter where in the world you live, at some point you'll interface with someone who's grappling in the darkness.

The global effects of this affliction cannot be overemphasized. Depression has physical and practical ramifications far beyond a melancholy mood, and impairs the basic functions of living and thriving. The World Health Organization (WHO) ranks depression as the single largest contributor to disability worldwide.[7] In the US, depression incurs levels of disability similar to those accompanying arthritis, cardiovascular disease, and stroke.[8] In the worst cases, the disorder threatens survival; depression is the major cause of suicide deaths across the globe, responsible for eight hundred thousand tragedies per year.[9]

Such data should alert us to the real possibility that when we lead or participate in worship every Lord's Day, brothers and sisters among us may be struggling with life-threatening despair. For such individuals, getting out of bed to attend church may require exceptional effort. Compassion in such cases is paramount, as depression preferentially strikes those already vulnerable to the ravages of a fallen world. Young adults, those with less income, and people who are divorced, separated, or widowed are especially prone to the condition.[10] Those already suffering and without support can sink into a mire of mood and thought from which they cannot wrench themselves free.

Causes
The diagnosis we call *major depression* is probably an umbrella term, a catchall phrase encompassing multi-

ple related syndromes with similar effects but distinct causes.[11] Numerous neurobiological changes—far more complicated than a "chemical imbalance"—are at work to drag sufferers into despondency. These processes involve changes in large brain structures,[12] intricate cell pathways,[13] and even molecules communicating between individual nerve cells.[14] While we don't know in all cases whether these changes *cause* depression or arise as a *result* of the disorder, they hint at why sufferers struggle to recover. In depression, the architecture of our brains shifts, trapping us in the dark.

And yet, biology doesn't tell the entire story. Life circumstances also affect our minds and moods. A family predisposition combined with an environmental influence—a devastating life event, substance abuse, medications, a complicating illness, even a spiritual crisis—usually places a person at high risk for that first episode of depression.[15] Furthermore, the symptoms of depression are notoriously heterogeneous, and one person's experience may differ drastically from another's.[16]

For example, people with seasonal affective disorder, who contend with depression during the winter months, respond well to bright-light therapy, while those without this temporal pattern don't. Some sufferers struggle only mildly, while others find themselves incapacitated and unable to function in daily life.[17] In my own journey, *anhedonia*—the inability to glean joy from activities one loves—was unbearable, but others with whom I've spoken have lamented their difficulties to read and concentrate, or their struggles to get out of bed, or a persistent heaviness that wouldn't leave (as if lead encased their limbs).

Triggers may be obvious—the death of a loved one, the loss of a job, a broken relationship—but depression may also descend without any clear inciting event at all. My first—and worst—depressive episode occurred on the tails of a traumatic event that threw my faith into turmoil, but others arrived swift and sudden as an icy breeze, without clear triggers, striking without warning while I watched my kids at a playground or sipped coffee at a sun-soaked breakfast table. I felt as if a switch suddenly flipped in my mind, and as all color and feeling drained away, I looked skyward and prayed: "Oh Lord, please, no. Not this. Not again."

The important take-home messages are that (1) depression is associated with complex brain changes that impair concentration and mood, and (2) one person's experience may dramatically differ from another's. Loving the depressed begins with acknowledging that experiences can vastly differ, even while suffering in all cases is profound. Meeting people in their grief, listening to their unique narratives, and then offering the love and teaching of Christ can serve as lifelines when the shadows descend.

If you're suffering with depression, know that your unique experience doesn't make you "weak" or imply a meager faith. You are a bearer of God's image, worthy of love, struggling in a fallen world. Depression is complex, harrowing, and variable, and your suffering is real.

Characteristics

Despite variability in the causes and presentations of depression, its clinical criteria are well established. A diagnosis of depression requires that at least five of the following symptoms occur nearly daily for at least two weeks:[18]

- depressed mood (hopelessness, despair)*
- anhedonia (loss of pleasure in usual passions and activities)*

- weight loss/weight gain or change in appetite
- insomnia/hypersomnia
- psychomotor agitation/retardation (can't sit still or can't get moving)
- fatigue/loss of energy*
- feelings of worthlessness or guilt*
- inability to concentrate*
- recurrent thoughts of death or suicide

Of these symptoms, at least one must be depressed mood or anhedonia—that is, despair or lack of joy. Additionally, any symptom above marked with an asterisk (*) occurs in over 60 percent of cases.[19] Note the prevalence of depressed mood, anhedonia, loss of energy, and impaired concentration, all of which can lead to marked difficulty in functioning at work, in household duties, and in relationships. In the most severe cases, sufferers may become bedbound and fail to perform basic activities of living, including personal hygiene and nutrition.

Note also that inappropriate feelings of guilt and worthlessness are part of the disorder. Sufferers of depression often feel ashamed that they can't pull themselves out of their melancholy. Perceived stigma tempts them to hide their difficulties and in some cases interferes with relationships, work, and school because they avoid interactions out of shame and anticipated criticism.[20] Anxiety also accompanies depression in up to half of all cases.[21] By the very nature of the disorder, those suffering from depression often feel too guilty and afraid to admit their condition to others.

Treatment

Because guilt and stigma discourage many from seeking assistance,[22] too few sufferers of major depression receive the help they need. In a survey of 5.4 million adults in the US who reported an unmet need for mental health services, 8.2 percent did not seek treatment because they didn't want others to find out, 9.5 percent because "it might cause neighbors/community to have a negative opinion," and 9.6 percent due to concerns about confidentiality.[23] Some 28 percent believed they could handle their problems without treatment, and 22.8 percent didn't know where to go to receive it.[24] Such statistics reveal that the road to healing from depression slopes uphill, and many tread it alone.

The two mainstays of treatment for clinical depression are antidepressant medications and psychotherapy or counseling. While both avenues can provide life-giving support, neither offers a quick fix. While both play vital roles in recovery, neither diminishes the importance of spiritual disciplines for sufferers striving to reclaim their joy.

Some, like Sarah, may worry that reliance upon medications implies a paltry faith. Others confuse antidepressants with opioids and fear addiction. In an opposing scenario, our pain-averse culture, which prioritizes comfort and instant gratification, can mislead the suffering toward chemical prescriptions for normal, refining grief. Throughout, questions churn: Are antidepressants permissible? Are they sufficient? Does our need for them reflect a deficit in faith? How do they factor into means of grace with which God has blessed us such as prayer, study of the word, and counseling?

Antidepressants increase the concentration of neurotransmitters in the brain, but it's not exactly clear why such effects help in depression. Given what we know about the complexities of the disorder, it's no surprise antidepressants produce modest effects. Though these medications can promote crucial *improvements* in symptoms, when used alone they facilitate *full remission* only about half the time.[25] We glean from research that antidepressants typically *lessen* symptoms of depression after eight weeks of therapy.[26] That's good news for those clambering in the gloom, for whom even minor improvement can provide stability to engage with the world. But it doesn't mean antidepressants have earned a reputation as a miracle cure.

In fact, when sufferers muster the courage to pursue therapy, they can face a plodding and debilitating course. Sixty percent of people who start antidepressant medication suffer side effects of stomach upset, drowsiness, weight gain, sexual dysfunction, and anxiety.[27] Though some feel better within one to two weeks,[28] full remission from depression usually requires six to twelve weeks of therapy.[29] This delayed response means sufferers shoulder side effects while still immersed in despair. Unsurprisingly, the dropout rate for therapy is high, with many discontinuing antidepressants before symptoms resolve.[30] The delayed and variable effectiveness of treatment can worsen feelings of guilt. As Zack Eswine writes, "Because of this slowness or absence of cure, sufferers of depression must daily withstand voices of condemnation. After all, *Shouldn't you be over it by now?*"[31]

Taken in total, research on antidepressants supports their use as *one component* of a comprehensive approach. For mild depression, doctors often recommend counseling alone—without antidepressants—given the risks of side effects with medication.[32] For moderate to severe depression, however, combining medication and psychotherapy has been shown to be more effective than either treatment alone.[33]

No medication can sponge away the blackness in our hearts. But in his steadfast love and mercy, God has gifted us with the common kindness of medical science. In the right circumstances, when carefully combined with counseling and spiritual disciplines, antidepressants can ease some of us back into daylight. While we should never rely on medication exclusively, neither should we demonize those who use it as part of a comprehensive approach.

The second mainstay of treatment—psychotherapy and counseling—can be crucial to keeping depression at bay. Studies show antidepressants and psychotherapy have similar efficacy initially, but after treatment *ends,* those treated with antidepressants alone commonly relapse.[34] The benefits of psychotherapy, however, persist long after treatment stops. Dr. Karen Mason, professor of counseling and psychology at Gordon-Conwell Theological Seminary, has witnessed this phenomenon firsthand. "There's a biological vulnerability that antidepressants address, but people are also dealing with social and behavioral issues that reinforce their depression," she related to me in personal correspondence. "You might be on antidepressants alone for six months and find they help, but as soon as you stop them, you become depressed again because patterns of thinking are still there."

Antidepressants are often *necessary* to equip sufferers for the hard work of recovery, but they are not typically *sufficient*. While they can lift a person's darkened mood, full recovery also requires attention to elements that pharmacology can't penetrate: social support, patterns of thinking, habits, histories, and especially one's walk with Christ. While antidepressants improve neurotransmitter signaling, psychotherapy and counseling can help us navigate the social and cognitive barriers to recovery. A believing therapist can encourage a rich life of prayer and Bible intake, with support from the body of Christ, which are essential to usher us through the storm.

Though episodic, depression is often a lifelong burden, and too often we weather one storm only to encounter another. After one episode, the estimated rate of recurrence over two years is greater than 40 percent; after two episodes, the risk of recurrence within five years is 75 percent.[35] These numbers mean depression repeatedly taunts its victims over a lifetime. Sufferers gasp with relief when one episode releases them, but the risk of recurrence always lingers. Over time, the darkness inflicts a heavy toll. All-cause mortality is up to 100 percent greater,[36] and suicide incidence is 27 times greater in depression than in the general population.[37]

For those seeking to love the depressed, patience, understanding, and Christian hope are paramount. For those battling depression, it's critical not to isolate yourself out of shame, to dismiss struggles as a personality defect, or to reject help.

Biblical Understanding of Depression

Sarah's initial reluctance to divulge her depression stemmed in part from a perceived stigma against mental illness in her church. She recalled one occasion when a church leader said, "Depression isn't an issue for Christians." On another occasion, a member of her small group questioned how anyone who knew the gospel could struggle with grief and sadness.

Unfortunately, Sarah's experience isn't unique. On top of the burdens of despondency, hopelessness, and guilt that sufferers of depression already shoulder, too often interactions with those in the church cement fears about inadequate faith. Dr. Beverly Yahnke, executive director of the Lutheran Center for Spiritual Care and Counsel, describes this tendency:

> Far too many well-intentioned Christians are imbued with the conviction that strong people of faith simply don't become depressed. Some have come to believe that by virtue of one's baptism, one ought to be insulated from perils of mind and mood. Others whisper unkindly that those who cast their cares upon the Lord simply wouldn't fall prey to a disease that leaves its victims emotionally desolate, despairing and regarding suicide as a refuge and comfort—a certain means to stopping relentless pain.[38]

Echoing these observations, Zack Eswine writes:

> In the eyes of many people, including Christian people,
> depression signifies cowardice, faithlessness, or a bad
> attitude. Such people tell God in prayer and their
> friends in person that the sufferer of depression is soft
> or unspiritual.[39]

Such misconceptions about suffering's role in the
Christian life can dissuade those with depression from
seeking help. In some cases, theological misunderstand-
ings or unrepentant sin may indeed contribute to depression, as was true in my own case. Cultivating a deeper and
more robust understanding of God's attributes offered me
an anchor that was crucial to my recovery. But spiritual
factors don't mean depression and faith are mutually ex-
clusive; on the contrary, Scripture teaches us that disciple-
ship is costly, that sin still ravages the world, that deep,
penetrating pain exists (even for believers), and that God
works through such pain for good.

An understanding of these truths can guide sufferers
back to their hope in Christ when they need it most. In
Sarah's case, a gradual and careful walk through Scripture

with compassionate church leaders was life-giving. As she wrestled to see the realities of her depression through a biblical lens, Sarah learned to trust God's sovereignty and mercy, to express her despair through lament, and to lean upon the church for support.

No book of this length can comprehensively address a theology of suffering,[40] but I will highlight key passages and themes from Scripture that may offer solace, understanding, and hope. A biblical understanding of suffering—and the truth that even those with strong faith can flail in the darkness—can alleviate false guilt, encourage suffering people to seek counseling, and ease them back toward the light.

Trials Will Come

Christ triumphed over death (1 Cor. 15:55; 2 Tim. 1:10), and when he returns, all its wretched manifestations will wash away (Isa. 25:7–8; Rev. 21:4–5). But for *now*, we live in the wake of the fall, in a world where sin corrupts every molecule, cell, and wayward breeze (Rom. 8:19–22). Jesus warned us that tribulation and persecution would follow his disciples into the world (Matt. 16:24–25; John 1:10–11; 15:20; 16:33), but in the good news of salvation he provides, he also gives us living hope (1 Pet. 1:3–5), a sturdy limb to which we can cling when storms assail us. While we await Jesus's return, the storms still come. Their winds beat on, crippling our bodies. Their torrents can lash us, drowning us in misery. Yet in Christ, we need not be subdued. Though pelting hail still stings and can drive even faithful Christians into despondency, we cleave to the firm assurance of eternal life.

When we dismiss depression as a defect in faith, we forget that the Savior we treasure has also known crushing sorrow (Matt. 26:38; 27:46). Though he shared perfect communion with the Father, he was acquainted with grief (Isa. 53:3). Our Savior has walked in the shadows, and he can sympathize with us (Heb. 4:15). He *knows* our groanings, and in love he *bore* them for our sake. When we despair and can't see God, our identity in Christ—and God's love for us—remains untarnished.

The gospel promises not freedom from pain but an abundantly more precious gift: the assurance of God's love, which *prevails* over sin and *buoys* us through the tempests. Christ offers hope that transcends the crooked wantonness of this broken world. Suffering can bear down on us. Depression can crush even the faithful. But in Christ, nothing can separate us from God's love (Rom. 8:38–39).

God Meant It for Good

When we dismiss depression as an affliction of faithlessness, we can crush believers during their moments of need, and ignore God's refining work in these moments of despair. We serve a heavenly Father whose love and sovereignty are so great that he can work through our worst anguish for our good and his glory. Paul prayed three times that God would remove his "thorn in the flesh," but rather than relieving Paul's pain, the Lord replied, "My grace is sufficient for you, for my power is made perfect in weakness" (2 Cor. 12:9). Freedom from pain, though ideal in our eyes, may not always be our greatest good.

Though Todd Peperkorn writes of his ordeal with depression in harrowing detail, he also reflects with gratitude on how the Lord worked through his misery to strengthen his faith:

Overcoming depression is not a matter of "cheer up!" or "just have more faith and joy!" or some pious version of "get over it!" I knew the gospel. I knew all the

right answers. I had it all figured out and preached it
Sunday after Sunday. But our Lord, in his mercy, chose
to crush me, to cause me to suffer with him, so that
the faith he gave me . . . would be stronger, clearer,
and more focused. By traveling down that dark road,
I have come to understand what the light of Christ
is all about.[41]

Just as the Lord refined Peperkorn through suffering,
he also drew me to himself through my bleakest hours.
Before depression struck, I strutted blithely through life
with a hardened, unexamined heart and sought meaning through my accomplishments rather than through
Christ. Just as the obstinate Jonah wouldn't open his lips
in prayer until locked within the gloom of a fish's belly,
I refused to gaze heavenward until driven to my knees,
enshrouded in despair I couldn't escape. While I would
never wish to return to that desolate place, I am thankful
for how God worked through the ordeal to sanctify me.
Only when I was desperate for God's light did he choose
to reveal himself to me through Scripture.

When discussing God's sovereignty, we must be careful
not to presume that suffering strikes people as a punish-

ment for weak faith. If we do, we err like Job's "miserable comforters" (Job 16:2), who wrongfully accused him of unrepentant sin. While God may allow us to suffer—to discipline us or to heighten our sense of reliance upon him for life, and breath, and everything (Acts 17:25)—he does not condemn us to depression as punishment for sin. Christ has already borne sin's penalty for us. His blood washes us whiter than snow (1 Cor. 6:11; Rev. 7:14).

Lest we doubt that God can work through our sorrows for good, we need only look to the cross. The Father sent his Son to bear the world's sufferings so we would have eternal life (Rom. 5:8; Eph. 2:4–9). Through Christ's suffering, God achieved history's most beautiful and magnificent act of grace. He saved us, giving us hope amid the despair that afflicts us this side of heaven, and when he returns, our salvation will be complete. He will wipe away every tear from our eyes.

How Long, O Lord?

Though those who suffer from depression may feel too embarrassed or ashamed to admit their condition, they may reap solace from the truth that they're not alone.

History and Scripture reveal that for centuries faithful Christ followers who have proclaimed God's goodness have also grappled with unshakable sorrow. Modern examples include Christian songwriters Michael Card and Andrew Peterson, who have both penned songs about their battles with depression.[42] These musicians follow in the footsteps of saints over the millennia. Charles Spurgeon fought depression all his life, once reflecting, "I could say with Job, 'My soul chooseth strangling rather than life.' I could readily enough have laid violent hands upon myself, to escape from my misery of spirit."[43] Even David, a man after God's own heart (1 Sam. 13:14), cried out to the Lord from the depths (Ps. 13:1–2). "All the day I go about mourning," he lamented.

> For my sides are filled with burning,
>> and there is no soundness in my flesh.
> I am feeble and crushed;
>> I groan because of the tumult of my heart.
>> (Ps. 38:6–8)

In fact, we see many vivid models of how to trust God through the cries of suffering in the Psalms. When depression seizes us, we too may perceive our days "like an evening shadow," and feel that we "wither away like grass" (Ps. 102:11). In Psalm 55, David grieves:

> My heart is in anguish within me;
>> the terrors of death have fallen upon me.
> Fear and trembling come upon me,
>> and horror overwhelms me. (vv. 4–5)

Such passages echo the turmoil within when depression obscures one's vision of Christ. As we fumble through the shadows in search of God, the Psalms reassure us that even those dearest to him endure such seasons. Those who have known and loved God have also drowned in anguish and cried out in longing for him.

Cling to the Light: How to Cope as a Sufferer

Dear friend, if you are among those who cry out to God and yearn for his comfort, *know you are not alone.* Your walk in the darkness cannot hide you from the light of the world (John 8:12). Even when you cannot feel his presence, Jesus remains with you until the end of the age (Matt. 28:20), and nothing—not your shame, despair, or the agony of depression—can separate you from his love (Rom. 8:38–39).

Though every hour may seem hopeless and every day a painful ordeal, healing *is* possible. The following practical guidelines can ease you toward a place of greater wholeness. Keep in mind these suggestions do not take the place of professional counseling.

Confide in Someone You Trust
When we struggle with depression, we often feel isolated and alone. We fear others won't understand our difficulties and will condemn us for our inability to "pull ourselves up by our bootstraps," and so while we thirst for companionship, our shame silences us. But when flailing in the dark, we need the guiding hand of fellowship more than ever.

Though fears of rejection may haunt you, identify people in your life whom you trust, and then confide in them about your struggles. Biblical counselor Ed Welch advises:

> "Tell someone you are depressed." That is a small, risky yet doable step. It might feel like you are coming out of hiding and acknowledging something hideous or shameful. But tell someone. If you have no idea who

to tell, tell your pastor. Among those who responded [to our survey about depression], there was a chorus that never stopped singing the same refrain: "Don't isolate. Don't isolate."[44]

Honestly sharing your struggles helps others to better love you and helps you to remain engaged. Safe people may include immediate family, a dear friend, a mentor, a counselor, or especially the church. Know that the body of Christ is designed to bear one another's burdens (Gal. 6:2), and connect with your pastor or members of your church who can weep alongside you (Rom. 12:5). As you voice your pain, invite others to pray with and for you. Private prayer may feel laborious, but requests on our behalf can provide a balm for our weary souls. No matter whom you invite into your confidence, be forthright about what helps and what makes days worse. Allowing others to be present with you without pretending all is well can give you freedom to heal.

Seek (and Accept!) Help
Depression is much more serious than a glum mood, and an early step toward shaking away the shadows and

reclaiming your joy is to acknowledge you need help. You can't overcome this affliction alone.

The first stop when seeking help for depression is your primary doctor's office, but it shouldn't be the last. While a family doctor determines whether an antidepressant will help, it's critically important to couple any medication with counseling. Your doctor may refer you to a psychiatrist or clinical psychologist, or alternatively you can seek out a Christian counselor through various on-line resources like Anchored Hope (anchoredhope.co), which provides clinically informed biblical counseling remotely. Additionally, both the American Association of Christian Counselors (AACC, www.aacc.net) and the Christian Counseling and Educational Foundation (CCEF, www.ccef.org) host helpful search engines with contact information for Christian counselors across the country.

If a doctor recommends antidepressants, don't view this as a failure. Such medications can be a crucial component of recovery, especially when combined with counseling. Though getting out the door to an appointment can feel impossible at times, aim to continue therapy as best you can. If you don't connect with or grow to trust the first counselor you see, seek out another therapist rather than abandoning treatment completely. Recruit a trusted friend to help you research options and to drive you to and from appointments. Lean on others to ease the burden and keep you accountable when your motivation is at a minimum.

Focus on Doing the Next Thing

Depression can feel like a mire of meaninglessness, but daily structure can keep you moving forward, even when your mind and body want to surrender. Elisabeth Elliot, a missionary well versed with suffering, relied upon an old Saxon poem to prod her to "do the next thing":

> Do it immediately; do it with prayer;
> Do it reliantly, casting all care;
> Do it with reverence, tracing His hand
> Who placed it before thee with earnest command.
> Stayed on omnipotence, safe 'neath His wing,
> Leave all resultings, DO THE NEXT THING.[45]

Doing the next thing can offer a lifeline in depression. The next thing need not be momentous. It may be the only task your mind can handle in the given instance—getting out of bed, making lunch, calling a friend, taking a walk, or driving to work. In her book on grief, Clarissa Moll reframes the daily routines of "eat, sleep, exercise" as "nourish, rest, move."[46] The words mean the same, but hers can seem less daunting to a weary heart. When simple tasks seem arduous, focus not on the responsibilities that loom but only on *the next thing*: nourish, rest, move. Repeat. As much as possible, incorporate these into routines to conserve your energy and limit the burden of daily decisions.

Lean into Prayer

Depression muddies concentration. We may yearn for God's word but find that our eyes gloss over familiar verses without comprehending them. Our hearts cry out for help, but we can't organize our anguish into a coherent prayer.

The Psalms are life-giving in such moments. When you're feeling well, bookmark particular psalms in your Bible to which you can turn when the fog of depression again clouds your thinking. When you're sinking into the depths, allow the psalms to anchor your prayers. Recite them as if they were your own words. If the Spirit moves you, add your own language of lament, pouring out your woes to God. Even if your prayers dwindle to single phrases—"Lord, have mercy on me"; "Father, please help me"—lift them up. God hears our prayers (1 John 5:15), and when our own words fail, the Spirit speaks on our behalf "with groanings too deep for words" (Rom. 8:26).

Guide to the Light: How Friends and Church Leaders Can Help

For Christ's followers, the call to love our neighbors is clear (Mark 12:31; John 13:34–35). We leap into the mission field, cook meals for the poor, and embrace the grieving because Scripture guides us to have special concern for the downtrodden and afflicted, to bear one another's burdens with joy (Mic. 6:8; Matt. 5:7; Gal. 6:2, 9–10; Phil. 2:4).

But when depression strikes a friend or loved one, the best way to help can elude us. We may worry we'll say the wrong thing and worsen someone's hopelessness. We may think depression is a medical condition outside our scope or assume sufferers will reach out if they desire help. Uncertain how to act, many don't act at all, lapsing into silence and avoidance.

But as stewards of the greatest message of hope in history, Christians are uniquely positioned to minister to those grappling with depression. Sufferers may know the gospel, but oftentimes they cannot feel its import for their daily lives. They may recite the Lord's Prayer, but the words have no effect when their hearts are heavy and awash in gray. In such circumstances, sufferers need Christian hope and reminders of God's love more than ever. The following encouragements can equip you to support the depressed, love them, and remind them of their hope in Christ in their dire need.

Stay Connected

Shame, exhaustion, and the presumption that few understand can drive those with depression into isolation. This tendency can entrench sufferers in misery, leaving them feeling more alone, forgotten, and unloved.

If you learn someone is battling depression, show him or her the face of Christ by staying connected. Don't wait for depressed individuals to reach out for help; odds are they won't, even if they desperately need support. Instead, offer to visit, pray over the phone, or bring groceries or a meal. Invite them out for a walk or over for dinner.

Check in regularly. Show them they're not alone, they're loved, and they have dignity and value.

In conversations, withhold judgmental comments. If a sufferer confides in you, it's crucial to recognize the difficulty of that admission and to respond gently, patiently, and without reproach. Listen and focus on a ministry of presence, following the sufferer's lead as to what helps and what doesn't. Some will welcome speaking openly about their ordeal with someone who listens and withholds condemnation. Others will relish diversion, a return to the activities and topics that once brought them joy. Still more will value being seen and esteemed as worthy of time and attention. Approach depression as a common reality in this sin-sickened world rather than as a problem unique to the sufferer alone.

Practice empathy and compassion. When Ed Welch conducted a survey of 365 people with depression and asked their thoughts about which people were most helpful, he found the ones deemed safe had a common profile:

They did not prejudge depression as wrong or a sign of spiritual weakness, they did not act like hired consultants who dispensed simple remedies, and they were willing to make time. A number of people wrote that they especially valued those who cared even without words—by a hug, a walk, or simply being present.[47]

If you discern patterns of unrepentant sin or faulty theology contributing to a sufferer's depression, address these gently. Partner and guide, rather than reprimanding. Offer to go to a counselor with the sufferer. Rather than recommending exercise, invite the person out for a walk. Read and unpack pertinent Bible passages together, both of you stooped over the text, rather than suggesting that a sufferer study on his or her own. Come alongside the hurting, reinforcing that they are not alone, and reassuring them you come not to heap on guilt and shame but to help bear their burdens (Gal. 6:2).

Pray Together

Those with depression often find prayer essential, yet arduous. Hopelessness and impaired concentration can cloud the mind, reducing prayers to just a single word or phrase.

Praying for and with the depressed can offer them a priceless gift. Bring them before the throne of grace in your personal devotions. When you visit with sufferers, offer to pray, and invite them to join you as they feel comfortable. Pray for their healing, for their perseverance, and for the truth that nothing can wrench them from God's love to penetrate their hearts.

Read Scripture Together

Often when sufferers seek out medical and counseling support, and labor to complete mundane tasks, they have little strength left to pore over Scripture. Words can fall limply, like withered leaves on the mind.

To support sufferers, offer to read Scripture with them. Keep in mind that impaired concentration abounds in depression. I relish studying the Bible, but in times of depression, reading seems impossible. My eyes scan the words, but the meaning evades me. This is not the time for extensive exegesis but for "slow listening" to God's word to hear even one thing that is good for your soul.[48] Passages that highlight Christ's redeeming work and God's promise of salvation can offer a lifeline when living feels like dying. Even single verses written on a slip of paper and kept in a pocket can help to usher a sufferer through the hard days. As one respondent to

Ed Welch's survey wrote, "I have to remind myself that God loves me every day, and pray every day, whether I feel like it or not."[49]

As I wrote above, the Psalms offer especially rich reassurances for those fighting depression. While I've lacked the clarity to study Scripture in depth during my depressive episodes, I've learned to earmark key psalms when I am well—especially the psalms of lament—so I know where to turn if I again sink into melancholy. For those waiting for the Lord "more than watchmen for the morning" (Ps. 130:6), guidance through the Psalms can bring welcome encouragement.

Encourage Professional Help

Misplaced guilt may compel sufferers to chastise themselves to "just get over it" on their own and to avoid seeking help, but as we've seen, the risks to well-being and even life itself are high without treatment. If a sufferer is meandering through an illness unguided, encourage him or her to seek professional assistance.

The road to treatment, as with so much else in depression, is tortuous. Many muster the courage to seek therapy, only to find an abundance of roadblocks: scarce providers, poor access to biblically grounded counseling, inadequate insurance, long waiting lists, and troubling side effects to medication. As mentioned above, a primary care doctor's office often constitutes the first stop on the road to treatment, but too often it also remains the last, with an antidepressant prescription the only help offered. If this is the case with someone you know, encourage your friend to seek out psychotherapy or Christian counseling from one of the organizations listed above (p. 30).

When Sorrow Turns Deadly: How to Prevent Suicide

In the worst cases of depression, suffering is so profound and seemingly inescapable that death seems the only possible relief. Millions[50] of people in the US struggle with thoughts of taking their own lives every year and, tragically enough, follow through to make suicide the twelfth leading cause of death in the US.[51] In 2020, 1.2 million Americans attempted suicide, and 45,979 succeeded.[52]

Despite these unsettling statistics, disciples of Christ have cause for hope. Church attendance and religious belief have both been linked to a lower risk of suicide.[53] Additionally, with help, most who survive a suicide attempt reach a place of hope and thriving.[54] This means prevention is critical. So how do we recognize a threat of suicide, and how do we intervene?

Stay Connected (Again!)

Love for my husband thwarted my suicidal plans, and as it happens, my situation is common. People struggling with suicidal thoughts are less likely to take their lives if they can identify a reason to live, especially if that reason involves relationships with others. People who are suicidal are often desperately lonely, and in fact, social isolation is a *risk factor* for death by suicide. Suicide prevention begins with caring enough about our friends and family to notice when something goes awry.

Recognize the Signs

While the likelihood of suicide is notoriously hard to predict, certain populations are at higher risk. People struggling with hopelessness and mental health challenges are vulnerable, especially if they have means of hurting themselves and scant support. Such high-risk groups include those suffering from abuse and trauma, veterans, rural and indigenous communities, middle-aged adults, and those struggling with gender dysphoria or same-sex attraction.[55] Recently, suicidal thoughts have markedly increased among young adults, especially young women.[56]

How do we know if someone in our midst is contemplating suicide? While discerning the signs can be difficult, certain changes in the behavior of a church member, friend, or loved one should raise concern. If someone's depression seems to worsen, and you notice the person socially withdrawing and neglecting hygiene, lovingly invite him or her into a conversation. Agitation and reckless behavior, especially if it involves increased substance abuse, can also hint that someone is veering toward self-harm. Other sufferers may suddenly have a brightening of their mood and give away all their prized possessions; this may reflect sudden resolve to commit suicide. Most ominous are ruminations about death, threats to commit suicide, and the active seeking of the means to take one's life. If you notice any of these behaviors, have a caring conversation immediately.

Have a Conversation

We may worry that asking someone about suicidal thoughts will put the idea in a sufferer's head, but studies show this concern is unfounded.[57] In fact, experts agree that the safest approach toward helping someone at risk for suicide is *directly asking*.

If someone's behavior concerns you, speak with him in private. Focus on the ministry of presence; seek to listen, and don't minimize his pain. Respect his privacy. However, if he admits to suicidal thoughts, kindly but firmly decline to keep his admission a secret. Instead, come alongside him and guide him toward professional help.

Determine Severity and Seek Help

If someone describes suicidal thoughts, it's crucial to distinguish between *passive* and *active* suicidal ideation. In passive suicidal ideation, the risk of immediate harm is lower, while those with active suicidal ideation need urgent help. To differentiate between these two patterns, ask individuals whether they have a *plan*, the *means*, and the *intent* to commit suicide.

Someone with passive suicidal ideation will make generic statements about wanting to die—for example, "I wish I would go to sleep and never wake up," or "I just want it all to be over." On further inquiry, however, these individuals don't have an express plan, means, or intent to act upon these suicidal thoughts. The best course of action in these cases is prompt referral to a licensed professional. Once again, come alongside sufferers, rather than offering advice. Instead of making suggestions, help the troubled person find a counselor or therapist, and offer to accompany him or her to the first appointment.

By contrast, someone with active suicidal ideation will have a plan to commit suicide, the means to do it (e.g., firearms or medication), and an intent to follow through. Someone expressing such thoughts *needs immediate hospitalization*. If you're not sure, err on the side of caution, and *do not leave the person alone*. Call or text the 988 Suicide and Crisis Lifeline at 988 to connect to a crisis counselor, and escort the sufferer to the emergency room. Find further help at the 988 Lifeline website (https://988lifeline.org) or the Suicide Prevention Resource Center (www.sprc.org).

A Living Hope

My prayer is that when gloom descends on the vulnerable, and living seems unbearable, the body of Christ will offer a cool cup of water. When we bolster one another with the message of God's grace and cleave to one another as brothers and sisters, we chase away the loneliness. We affirm our hope, not in the work of our meager hands but in Christ, through whom God shows his boundless love, mercy, and forgiveness. And in the face of that love, pinpricks of light penetrate the darkness.

Acknowledgments

PORTIONS OF THIS BOOKLET draw from these previously published articles by Kathryn Butler, with permission:

"How the Church Can Help in Suicide Prevention." TGC. May 7, 2021. https://www.thegospel coalition.org/.

"Out of the Depths I Cry to You: Turning to Psalms in Depression." Desiring God. August 26, 2017. https://www.desiringgod.org/.

"Scrambling for the Light: Christian Depression and the Use of Medication." Desiring God. May 15, 2019. https://www.desiringgod.org/.

"Truths the Church Needs to Realize about Suicide." Lifeway Research. September 23, 2022. https://

research.lifeway.com/2022/09/23/5-truths-the
-church-needs-to-realize-about-suicide.

"Why Christian Love Matters in Depression." TGC.
July 24, 2018. https://www.thegospelcoalition
.org/.

Notes

1. Todd A. Peperkorn, *I Trust When Dark My Road: A Lutheran View of Depression* (St. Louis, MO: LCMS, 2009), 9.

2. Charles H. Spurgeon, "Psalm 88," in *The Treasury of David*, The Spurgeon Archive, http://archive.spurgeon .org/treasury/ps088.php, accessed April 18, 2023.

3. Deborah Hasin et al., "Epidemiology of Adult DSM-5 Major Depressive Disorder and Its Specifiers in the United States," *JAMA Psychiatry* 75, no. 4 (2018): 336–46.

4. World Health Organization (WHO), *Depression and Other Common Mental Disorders: Global Health Estimates* (Geneva: World Health Organization, 2017), 5.

5. Graham Thornicroft et al., "Undertreatment of People with Major Depressive Disorder in 21 Countries," *British Journal of Psychiatry* 210, no. 2 (2017): 119–24.

6. Ronald C. Kessler et al., "Development of Lifetime Comorbidity in the World Health Organization World Mental Health Surveys," *Archives of General Psychiatry* 68, no. 1 (2011): 90–100.

7. WHO, *Depression*, 5.

8. Kirsten Penner-Goeke et al., "Reductions in Quality of Life Associated with Common Mental Disorders: Results from a Nationally Representative Sample," *Journal of Clinical Psychiatry* 76, no. 11 (2015): 1506–12.

9. WHO, *Depression*, 5.

10. Hasin et al., "Epidemiology," 336.

11. Gordon Parker, "The Benefits of Antidepressants: News or Fake News?," *British Journal of Psychiatry* 213, no. 2 (2018): 454–55.

12. P. Cédric M. P. Koolschijn et al., "Brain Volume Abnormalities in Major Depressive Disorder: A Meta-Analysis of Magnetic Resonance Imaging Studies," *Human Brain Mapping* 30, no. 11 (2009): 3719–35.

13. Roselinde H. Kaiser et al., "Large-Scale Network Dysfunction in Major Depressive Disorder: A Meta-Analysis of Resting-State Functional Connectivity," *Journal of the American Medical Association: Psychiatry* 72, no. 6 (2015): 603–11.

14. F. M. Werner and R. Coveñas, "Classical Neurotransmitters and Neuropeptides Involved in Major Depression: A Multi-Neurotransmitter System," *Journal of Cytology & Histology* 5, no. 4 (2014): 4853–58.

15. Patrick F. Sullivan, Michael C. Neale, and Kenneth S. Kendler, "Genetic Epidemiology of Major Depression: Review and Meta-Analysis," *American Journal of Psychiatry* 157, no. 10 (2000): 1552–62.

16. Eiko I. Fried and Randolph M. Nesse, "Depression Is Not a Consistent Syndrome: An Investigation of Unique Symptom Patterns in the STAR*D Study," *Journal of Affective Disorders*, 172 (2015): 96–102.

17. Jeffrey J. Rakofsky et al., "The Prevalence and Severity of Depressive Symptoms along the Spectrum of Unipolar Depressive Disorders: A Post Hoc Analysis," *Journal of Clinical Psychiatry* 74, no. 11 (2013): 1084–91.

18. "Depressive Disorders," in *DSM-5-TR*, DSM Library, https://doi.org/10.1176/appi.books.9780890425787.x04_Depressive_Disorders, accessed April 27, 2023.

19. Rakofsky et al., "Prevalence and Severity," 1088.

20. Antonio Lasalvia et al., "Global Pattern of Experienced and Anticipated Discrimination Reported by People

with Major Depressive Disorder: A Cross-Sectional Survey," *Lancet* 381, no. 9860 (2013): 55–62.

21. Bruce A. Arnow et al., "Depression Subtype in Predicting Antidepressant Response: A Report from the iSPOT-D Trial," *American Journal of Psychiatry* 172, no. 8 (2015): 743–50.

22. Thornicroft et al., "Undertreatment," 122.

23. Substance Abuse and Mental Health Services Administration (SAMHSA), *Results from the 2012 National Survey on Drug Use and Health: Mental Health Findings* (Rockville, MD: HHS, 2013), 24.

24. SAMHSA, *2012 National Survey*, 24.

25. Gerald Gartlehner et al., "Comparative Benefits and Harms of Second-Generation Antidepressants for Treating Major Depressive Disorder: An Updated Meta-Analysis," *Annals of Internal Medicine* 155, no. 11 (2011): 772–85.

26. Andrea Cipriani et al., "Comparative Efficacy and Acceptability of 21 Antidepressant Drugs for the Acute Treatment of Adults with Major Depressive Disorder: A Systematic Review and Network Meta-Analysis," *Lancet* 391, no. 10128 (2018): 1357–66.

27. Gartlehner et al., "Comparative Benefits and Harms," 772.

NOTES TO PAGES 15–16

28. Rudolf Uher et al., "Early and Delayed Onset of Response to Antidepressants in Individual Trajectories of Change During Treatment of Major Depression: A Secondary Analysis of Data from the Genome-Based Therapeutic Drugs for Depression (GENDEP) Study," *Journal of Clinical Psychiatry* 72, no. 11 (2011): 1478–84.

29. George I. Papakostas, "Managing Partial Response or Nonresponse: Switching, Augmentation, and Combination Strategies for Major Depressive Disorder," *Journal of Clinical Psychiatry* 70, suppl. 6 (2009): 16–25.

30. Gartlehner et al., "Comparative Benefits and Harms," 774.

31. Zack Eswine, *Spurgeon's Sorrows: Realistic Hope for Those Who Suffer from Depression* (Fearn, Ross-shire, UK: Christian Focus, 2014), 58.

32. National Institute for Health and Clinical Excellence, "Depression in Adults: Treatment and Management," *Guideline NG222*, June 29, 2022.

33. Pim Cuijpers et al., "Adding Psychotherapy to Pharmacotherapy in the Treatment of Depressive Disorders in Adults: A Meta-Analysis," *Journal of Clinical Psychiatry* 70, no. 9 (2009): 1219–29.

34. Alan J. Gelenberg et al., *Practice Guideline for the Treatment of Patients with Major Depressive Disorder*, 3rd ed. (Washington, DC: American Psychiatric Association, 2010), 47–49.

35. David A. Solomon et al., "Multiple Recurrences of Major Depressive Disorder," *American Journal of Psychiatry* 157, no. 2 (2000): 229–333.

36. Thomas Munk Laursen et al., "Mortality and Life Expectancy in Persons with Severe Unipolar Depression," *Journal of Affective Disorders* 193 (2016): 203–7.

37. F. Angst et al., "Mortality of Patients with Mood Disorders: Follow-Up over 34–38 Years," *Journal of Affective Disorders* 68, nos. 2–3 (2002): 167–81.

38. Beverly K. Yahnke, introduction to *Dark My Road*, by Peperkorn, 5.

39. Eswine, *Spurgeon's Sorrows*, 58.

40. For a more complete exposition, see C. S. Lewis, *The Problem of Pain* (1940; repr., New York: HarperOne, 2015); Timothy Keller, *Walking with God through Pain and Suffering* (New York: Penguin, 2013); and John Piper and Justin Taylor, *Suffering and the Sovereignty of God* (Wheaton, IL: Crossway, 2006).

41. Peperkorn, *Dark My Road*, 10.

42. Andrew Peterson, "The Rain Keeps Falling," track 5 on *The Burning Edge of Dawn* (Centricity Music, 2015); Michael Card, "The Edge," track 8 on *Poiéma* (Sparrow Records, 1994).

43. Charles H. Spurgeon, *The Metropolitan Tabernacle Pulpit Sermons*, vol. 36 (London: Passmore and Alabaster, 1890), 200.

44. Ed Welch, "Enduring in the Midst of Depression," CCEF, July 14, 2022, https://www.ccef.org/enduring -in-the-midst-of-depression/.

45. Elisabeth Elliot, "Loneliness: Do the Next Thing," *Gateway to Joy*, November 21, 1988, https://elisabethelliot .org/; the Elisabeth Elliot Foundation newsletter, Spring 2022, PDF.

46. Clarissa Moll, *Beyond the Darkness: A Gentle Guide for Living with Grief and Thriving after Loss* (Carol Stream, IL: Tyndale, 2022), 60.

47. Welch, "Enduring."

48. Welch, "Enduring."

49. Welch, "Enduring."

50. "Suicide Statistics," American Foundation for Suicide Prevention (AFSP), https://afsp.org/suicide-statistics/, accessed April 27, 2023.

51. Matthew F. Garnett, Sally C. Curtin, and Deborah M. Stone, "Suicide Mortality in the United States, 2000–2020," in *NCHS Data Brief*, no. 433 (Hyattsville, MD: National Center for Health Statistics, 2022); Centers for Disease Control and Prevention, March 3, 2022, https://www.cdc.gov/nchs/.

52. AFSP, "Suicide Statistics."

53. Karen Mason, *Preventing Suicide: A Handbook for Pastors, Chaplains, and Pastoral Counselors* (Downers Grove, IL: InterVarsity Press, 2014), 38.

54. "What We've Learned through Research," American Foundation for Suicide Prevention, https://afsp.org/what-we-ve-learned-through-research, accessed April 27, 2023.

55. "Disparities in Suicide," Centers for Disease Control and Prevention, https://www.cdc.gov/, accessed April 27, 2023.

56. "Youth Risk Behavior Survey: Data Summary and Trends Report, 2009–2019," Centers for Disease Control and Prevention, https://www.cdc.gov/healthyyouth/data/yrbs/pdf/YRBSDataSummaryTrendsReport2019-508.pdf, 59, accessed April 27, 2023.

57. Mary Kate Law et al., "Does Assessing Suicidality Frequently and Repeatedly Cause Harm? A Randomized Control Study," *Psychological Assessment* 27, no. 4 (2015): 1171–81.

Recommended Resources

Butler, Kathryn. *Glimmers of Grace: A Doctor's Reflections on Faith, Suffering, and the Goodness of God.* Wheaton, IL: Crossway, 2019. In this book, I share my firsthand experiences as a trauma surgeon, walking alongside patients, colleagues, and friends through various illnesses and aching loss. These hardships aren't limited to physical problems; often when our bodies are in pain, our spiritual lives can suffer too.

Eswine, Zack. *Spurgeon's Sorrows: Realistic Hope for Those Who Suffer from Depression.* Fearn Ross-Shire, UK: Christian Focus, 2014. In this winsome and insightful book, Eswine invites readers into Charles Spurgeon's experiences with depression, offering the hurting a compassionate hand and "a handwritten note of one who wishes you well."

Mason, Karen. *Preventing Suicide: A Handbook for Pastors, Chaplains, and Pastoral Counselors.* Downers Grove, IL: InterVarsity Press, 2014. Featuring thorough research and wisdom she's attained through decades of counseling experience, Mason provides a practical guide to help church leaders recognize the signs of suicidal thoughts and guide sufferers to lifesaving help.

Moll, Clarissa. *Beyond the Darkness: A Gentle Guide for Living with Grief and Thriving after Loss.* Carol Stream, IL: Tyndale, 2022. In this tender, poignant book, Moll shares insights she learned after the unexpected death of her husband. Though she primarily discusses bereavement and grief, her delicate prose, heart for Christ, and gentle advice will offer healing and guidance for those suffering from depression as well.

Peperkorn, Todd A., *I Trust When Dark My Road: A Lutheran View of Depression.* St. Louis, MO: LCMS, 2009. Raw, honest, heartbreaking, and revealing, Peperkorn's memoir on depression guides readers into the struggles of one grappling in the dark from the perspective of one who knows and loves Christ.

Scripture Index

1 Samuel
13:14 26

Job
3 2
16:2 25

Psalms
book of. 26, 27,
                        32, 38
13:1–2 26
13:1–3 2
22:1–2 2
38:6–8 26
55:4–5 27
69:1–3 2
102:11 27
130:6 38

Isaiah
25:7–8 21
53:3 . . . . 3, 22

Micah
6:8 33

Matthew
5:7 33
16:24–25 21
26:36–46 3
26:38 22
27:46 22
28:20 27

Mark
12:31 33

Luke
19:41–42 2

John
1:10–11 21
8:12 27
11:33–36 2
13:34–35 33
15:20 21
16:33 21

Acts
17:25 25

Romans
5:8 25
8:19–22 21
8:26 33
8:38–39 .... 23, 28
12:5 29

1 Corinthians
6:11 25
15:55 21

2 Corinthians
12:9 23

Galatians
6:2 .... 29, 33,
                          36
6:9–10 33

Ephesians
2:4–9 25

Philippians
2:4 33

2 Timothy
1:10 21

Hebrews
4:15 22

1 Peter
1:3–5 22

1 John
5:15 33

Revelation
7:14 25
21:4–5 21

TGC | THE GOSPEL COALITION

The Gospel Coalition (TGC) supports the church in making disciples of all nations, by providing gospel-centered resources that are trusted and timely, winsome and wise.

Guided by a Council of more than 40 pastors in the Reformed tradition, TGC seeks to advance gospel-centered ministry for the next generation by producing content (including articles, podcasts, videos, courses, and books) and convening leaders (including conferences, virtual events, training, and regional chapters).

In all of this we want to help Christians around the world better grasp the gospel of Jesus Christ and apply it to all of life in the 21st century. We want to offer biblical truth in an era of great confusion. We want to offer gospel-centered hope for the searching.

Join us by visiting TGC.org so you can be equipped to love God with all your heart, soul, mind, and strength, and to love your neighbor as yourself.

TGC.org

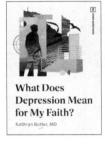

Also Available from the Gospel Coalition

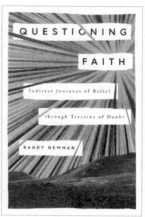